100

THINGS TO DO IN

OAKLAND

BEFORE YOU

DIE

100

THINGS TO DO IN
OAKLAND
BEFORE YOU
DIE

• • • • • • • • • • • • • • • • • • • •

JESSIE FETTERLING

REEDY PRESS

Permissions may be sought directly from Reedy Press at the above mailing address or via
our website at www.reedypress.com.

Library of Congress Control Number: 2017934536

ISBN: 9781681060972

Design by Jill Halpin

Printed in the United States of America
17 18 19 20 21 22   5 4 3 2

Please note that websites, phone numbers, addresses, and company names are subject to
change or cancellation. We did our best to relay the most accurate information available, but
due to circumstances beyond our control, please do not hold us liable for misinformation.
When exploring new destinations, please do your homework before you go.

DEDICATION

For my father, Stephen Fetterling,
who encouraged me to move to California and achieve my
dreams—love you always fella. And to the 36 people who lost
their lives in the 2016 Ghost Ship warehouse fire.
This book is dedicated to honor the memory of all of you.

Photo Credit:
Jason Lew
Courtesy of Oakland Museum of California

CONTENTS

Music and Entertainment

• •

Sports and Recreation

Culture and History

● ●

Shopping and Fashion

• •

PREFACE

Oakland is in the middle of a renaissance and has quickly become a melting pot for hipsters, techies, and aspiring artists escaping the San Francisco fog. But at its heart are the families that have called this city home for decades, giving it a rare sense of community that's dying in other parts of the San Francisco Bay Area.

This can be experienced firsthand every month at Oakland First Fridays, where local bands and artists converge to put on the ultimate block party. The Grand Lake Farmers Market every Saturday provides another canvas for cultural and ethnic diversity. It only takes about ten minutes at one of these city-wide events to see how Oakland, the birthplace of the Black Panther Party and other social justice organizations, is the definition of civic pride, welcoming any and all who visit to feel at home.

After moving all around the Bay Area for six years, I, too, found that sense of home when I finally decided to plant my roots in downtown Oakland. Watching Oakland grow from a distance and from the center of it all has been something I've truly enjoyed. Narrowing my favorite things to do in this continually evolving city to just 100 was tough, but I chose these "things" based on the personal memories I've cherished and continue to have at each one. I hope you'll share in the fun of exploring this soulful city by visiting these 100 places and the many more that Oakland has to offer.

• •

ACKNOWLEDGMENTS

I wanted to say a special thanks to all the local establishments who generously shared their knowledge with me. Thank you to the hardworking team at Visit Oakland for all your guidance and support. I would be lost without the love and support of my mother, stepfather, brother and friends. Lastly, Stephane, thanks for always inspiring me to be a better version of myself.

• •

FOOD AND DRINK

DRINK A GREYHOUND
AT CAFE VAN KLEEF

Before the downtown food and drink scene really started to take off in recent years, there was always Cafe Van Kleef. Funky knickknacks and artwork—a rhino head on the wall and beads hanging from chandeliers—line the walls of this dark, narrow hangout. The bar's best highlight, however, is its famous greyhound cocktail. All night long, bartenders are tirelessly squeezing fresh grapefruit juice behind the bar as they cater to the customers salivating to get their hands on one of the famous vodka-grapefruit drinks, topped off with a generous slice of the citrusy fruit. The cocktail's so good, in fact, that it's been known to attract visitors from the *other* side of the Bay Bridge just to come in and have at least one or two. On weekend nights, the bar also has live music to keep the masses entertained into the wee hours.

1621 Telegraph Avenue
510-763-7711
cafevankleef.com

SLURP UP SOME RAMEN
AT SHINMAI

New to the Oakland ramen scene is Shinmai, the second Japanese restaurant from the owner of Kakui Sushi, located in the city's Montclair neighborhood. Shinmai, however, is the first in the area to meld authentic ramen with an izakaya-style dining experience. Think the Japanese version of an Irish pub or Spanish tapas spot. While the atmosphere is casual, the dim lighting and nondescript signage out front make it as trendy as it sounds. The ramens on the menu are both flavorful and can be made even more so with the addition of the spicy himitsu paste. The izakaya plates, however, are not to be missed, with highlights including fried potato salad and Thai coconut curry mussels. And don't forget to top off the meal with a tasty craft cocktail. A fan favorite is the Where's Valdez?—a delicious blend of mezcal, toasted brown rice syrup and firewater bitters, among other ingredients.

1825-3 San Pablo Avenue
510-271-1888
shinmaioakland.com

Photo Credit:
Colin Burke McClure

GRAB A PINT
AT THE TRAPPIST

The minute you step inside the Trappist, you feel as if you've crossed the Atlantic to enter a traditional European pub—rightfully so, since its design is modeled after the owner's favorite beer spots from abroad. While its interior offers cozy candlelight and a couple of different rooms to create more intimate nooks, the Belgian and specialty beer menu is what keeps people here. The bar has twenty-five rotating taps and a rotating bottle list of between eighty and one hundred specialty beers from all over the world, but particularly from Belgium, the Netherlands, Scandinavia, and the United States. Located inside an 1870s Victorian building in Old Oakland, this bar has stood the test of time as one of the staples in this historic neighborhood. Its patio space outside also creates a welcoming backyard vibe on a warm Oakland day, which can be made even more so with a cheese or meat board.

460 8th Street
510-238-8900
thetrappist.com

BRUNCH IT UP
AT THE TRUSTY OAKLAND GRILL

This breakfast hot spot is always busy on weekends, but the wait is surprisingly reasonable. Maybe it's because the food that walks by as you wait is so tantalizingly good that thirty minutes seems like three. The crab cake benedict is definitely a highlight, while the restaurant's scramble special always packs a flavorful punch. The brick interior and low-hanging lights create a warm, neighborhood feel—just what you want for a champagne brunch. That's right. Strawberry mimosas or glasses of champagne are available for cheap on weekends. The menu extends well beyond breakfast, too, with one of the most underrated burgers in town and a long list of delicious sandwiches and salads.

301 Franklin Street
510-835-1176
oaklandgrill.net

TIP

Another diner-style restaurant serving up delicious omelets and sandwiches—ahem, the croque monsieur—is Mama's Royal Café.

(Note: Checks and credit cards are "cheerfully" not accepted here.)

4012 Broadway, 510-547-7600, mamasroyalcafeoakland.com

SIT AROUND A FIRE PIT
AT DRAKE'S DEALERSHIP

With the city's recent tech boom came trendy restaurants, and top on that list is Drake's Dealership. The local Drake's Brewing Co. decided to set up shop inside a brick building that once was the parts and service department of an old Dodge dealership in the city's historic Broadway Auto Row. It's quickly become one of the city's most popular backyards, with a massive beer garden complete with fire pits, Adirondack chairs, and a live music stage for DJs that typically play Thursday through Saturday. The full-service restaurant serves up wood-fired pizza alongside the brewing company's thirty-two beers on tap, brewed in nearby San Leandro. Adventurous eaters should try the Frito pie, a delicate blend of Frito-Lay chips, flank steak chili, bacon fondue, cheddar, onion, and pickled peppers.

2325 Broadway
510-568-2739
drinkdrakes.com

STEP BACK IN TIME
AT HEINOLD'S FIRST AND LAST CHANCE

Opened in 1883 as J.M. Heinold's Saloon, this famous watering hole hasn't lost its original charm—so much so that the entire bar is on a tilt created from the 1906 San Francisco earthquake. Located in Jack London Square, the bar earned its current name in the 1920s when ferry commuters making their way to nearby Alameda (a dry city at the time) would visit for their first or last chance to have an adult beverage. Over time, servicemen would ship out from the Port of Oakland, and the bar's tradition continued. It is here, too, where author Jack London found inspiration for his adventure novels *The Sea Wolf* and *The Call of the Wild.* History aside, the staff still running this joint are welcoming and fun, even playing pranks on some of the patrons. If you're lucky, you'll get the opportunity to meet Murray, the doorman's giant dog that takes up about a tenth of the bar's space.

48 Webster Street
510-839-6761
heinoldsfirstandlastchance.com

EAT A
22-INGREDIENT SALAD
AT BURMA SUPERSTAR

Even though Burma Superstar's original location opened in San Francisco in 1992, the restaurant has since graced the East Bay with its presence by opening two locations: one in Oakland and the other in nearby Alameda. Situated in Temescal, the Oakland location is similar to its San Francisco counterpart in that it has a wait determined by a sign-in clipboard, which the staff checks whenever there's time. Once you're seated, though, it's so worth it. There's a reason why this Burmese restaurant has become a Bay Area cult food destination. Its rainbow salad alone has twenty-two ingredients, which is served so that you see each one before it's mixed right at the table. The noodles and rice dishes are equally delicious, with lots of coconut and curry flavors that blend together perfectly.

4721 Telegraph Avenue
510-652-2900
burmasuperstar.com

DON'T FORGO A SLICE OF PIE
AT LOIS THE PIE QUEEN

If you're looking for your grandma's Southern cooking, then take a step inside Lois the Pie Queen. Open most days from 8:00 a.m. to 2:00 p.m., the staff at this no-frills restaurant is even as welcoming as grandma would be, a tradition that Lois started when she opened the restaurant in 1951. (The establishment has since been taken over by her son, Chris.) The chicken and waffle is definitely a highlight on the menu, but restaurant goers can expect other Southern specialties, such as cornbread muffins, buttermilk biscuits, and even grits. Then, there's the pie. About twelve different pies are on the menu, but get there early to guarantee they don't sell out. Note: The restaurant is cash only.

851 60th Street
510-658-5616

ORDER A BLACK & TAN SUNDAE
AT FENTONS CREAMERY

This retro creamery is a nod to the soda fountain shops and ice cream parlors of yesteryear. In fact, the landmark institution got its start when E.S. Fenton first delivered dairy products by horse-drawn wagon in the Piedmont Avenue neighborhood, where the storefront still stands today. E.S.'s grandson, Melvin Fenton, was responsible for creating several of the creamery's favorite flavors: toasted almond, Swiss milk chocolate, and the world-renowned rocky road ice cream flavor. The creamery also doubles as a restaurant, serving up burgers and fries, but its black and tan sundae is the must-order. Toasted almond and vanilla flavors are layered with handmade caramel and chocolate fudge, topped with toasted almonds, whipped cream, and a cherry. This place is so nostalgic that it appeared in the motion picture *Up,* made by Pixar, a local production company. Curious patrons can also take the Arctic Tour of the facility to learn more about the handmade ice cream production process.

4226 Piedmont Avenue
510-658-7000
fentonscreamery.com

FEEL THE HEAT FROM THE OPEN FIRE
AT CAMINO

No one cooks over an open fire quite like Camino. Founded by husband/wife team Russell Moore and Allison Hopelain in 2008, this restaurant keeps it simple with three main courses crafted each night over three separate fires. At the helm is Moore, who trained at Alice Waters' Chez Panisse Restaurant just up the road, which means the menu is ingredient driven. Even spirits are not served here unless they can be traced back to the source. The restaurant's ambience carries no such pretension, however, with its brick walls, long wooden communal tables, and a wide-open kitchen. While the food is no joke, with each bite on your plate very much intentionally placed, its low-waste kitchen polices and no-tip system have given it notoriety as a socially responsible place to work—and eat.

3917 Grand Avenue
510-547-5035
caminorestaurant.com

MIX IT UP
AT MUA

Mua offers a lively, urban vibe from the very start with spray-painted letters on what looks like a garage door that illuminates the restaurant's Auto Row location at night. Situated in a warehouse-like space, the urban feel continues with high ceilings, communal tables, and chalk artwork lining the walls. It's the restaurant's menu, however, that really shows off its creativity by taking the shared plate concept and turning it on its head. Highlights include asparagus salad with potato, grapefruit, and grain mustard; no-cheese mac 'n' cheese using butternut squash; and 24-hour pork spare ribs featuring a distinct tangy barbecue sauce. The drink menu—with such items as a rosemary martini and ginger julep—also provides a new take on traditional cocktails. Even more urban—or oh so Oakland—the restaurant supports local artists with a rotating gallery of artwork every month, hosting First Friday events that coincide with the city's monthly street festival.

2442 Webster Street
510-238-1100
muaoakland.com

Three Other Places to Get Small Plates:

À Côté
5478 College Avenue
510-655-6469
acoterestaurant.com

Duende
468 19th Street
510-893-0174
duendeoakland.com

Shakewell
3407 Lakeshore Avenue
510-251-0329
shakewelloakland.com

PLAY OUTSIDE
AT LOST & FOUND

The Oakland beer scene has blown up as of late because of such spots as Lost & Found. This indoor/outdoor beer garden serves up an extensive beer list that includes everything from local craft beers to European imports. The menu changes with the seasons and pairs perfectly with a dose of the urban outdoors. The beer garden certainly plays up its "garden" description, with an outdoor space that almost doubles its indoor space. Umbrella-covered picnic tables, potted plants, graffiti artwork, and yard games such as Ping-Pong and cornhole, give it an in-your-own-backyard feel. As if it didn't have enough appeal already, Lost & Found also hosts special community events, such as record swaps and a monthly bazaar featuring local arts, crafts, and DIY trinkets.

2040 Telegraph Avenue
510-763-2040
lostandfound510.com

TASTE A SLICE OF ITALY
AT BOOT & SHOE SERVICE

The second of three restaurants opened by Charlie Hallowell, Boot & Shoe Service brings the best of the other two to the table, serving up fresh pizza pies like his first restaurant, Pizzaiolo, with the sleek atmosphere of his latest, Penrose. Another local chef to have trained in the kitchen at Chez Panisse, specifically at the helm of the restaurant's pizza oven, the locavore culture permeates the Italian kitchen at Boot & Shoe. Using ingredients sourced from local farms, the salads, pizzas, and pastas taste so fresh that you'd think you were in Italy. Add to that a delicious cocktail menu and U-shaped bar ideal for Friday-night conversations, and locals never seem to want to leave. Its café, outdoor patio, and brunch menu (on weekends only) also make it a fun daytime hangout.

3308 Grand Avenue
510-763-2668
bootandshoeservice.com

Charlie Hallowell's Two Other Restaurant Locations:

Pizzaiolo	Penrose
5008 Telegraph Avenue	3311 Grand Avenue
510-652-4888	510-444-1649
pizzaiolooakland.com	penroseoakland.com

ATTEMPT NEW FUSION DISHES
AT BLIND TIGER

Blind Tiger offers Asian fusion tapas that blend the culinary tastes from several cultures. Braised beef–topped curry fries. Asian chicken wings. Ramen macaroni and cheese. These are just a few of the treats offered in this underground restaurant. Very unassuming from its Telegraph Avenue entrance, patrons walk downstairs into an open space, decorated with Asian lanterns and wooden tree branches lining the ceiling. Cult movie classics, such as *The Big Lebowski,* are projected on the massive white screen that takes up a large part of one of the restaurant's walls. Communal wooden tables amplify the shared experience that will surely leave you licking your fingers when you're done.

2600 Telegraph Avenue
510-899-9694
blindtigeroakland.com

GET A LITTLE MESSY WITH SEAFOOD
FROM ALAMAR

Alamar provides a taste of New Orleans in downtown Oakland, with a make-your-own seafood boil option that's quintessential to the restaurant's experience. Choose from a variety of seafood, such as peel 'n' eat shrimp, pei mussels, or manila clams, and customize your boil with a house ragin' Cajun sauce. Then add in some extras, such as house sausage, corn on the cob, and baby red potatoes, for a traditional Cajun feast so good that it will leave you spooning the buttery remnants. (I know from firsthand experience.) While the seafood boils are a must, the restaurant offers other seafood treats, including oysters, poke bowls, and even fish tacos. Don't let the restaurant's varied menu items fool you, though. Its order-at-the-counter service makes it a quick meal for lunch or before a show at the nearby Fox or Paramount theaters.

100 Grand Avenue
510-907-7555
alamaroakland.com

CHALLENGE SOMEONE TO SHUFFLEBOARD
AT THE KINGFISH PUB & CAFE

The Kingfish Pub & Cafe is one of the oldest bars in Oakland, serving up booze and a friendly neighborhood vibe since 1922. This bar is so popular, in fact, that locals fought to keep it from being demolished, and its original structure was moved in 2015 to a new Telegraph Avenue location with an inviting patio. The shuffleboard and free popcorn continue to draw the regulars, while the bar's outdoor space has given it a new life, attracting a variety of patrons and their dogs to come sit beneath the patio's massive palm tree. TVs both inside and out make The Kingfish or simply "The Fish" an ideal spot to watch sports, while its reasonably priced drinks guarantee a Sunday Funday that can quickly lead into an evening.

5227 Telegraph Avenue
510-655-7373
kingfishpubandcafe.com

GET FANCY WITH A PRIX-FIXE MEAL
AT COMMIS

The only restaurant in Oakland to be honored with a coveted Michelin star—two to be exact—Commis sets the bar high for East Bay cuisine. Its eight-course, prix-fixe dinner rotates monthly, but a signature dish for Chef James Syhabout that continues to get rave reviews consists of a poached egg set atop a creamy allium puree with tastes of smoked dates and malt. This is served with the chef's famous baked sourdough bread—crunchy on the outside and warm and soft on the inside. While the ingredients are as simple as a global breakfast, their taste and cooked-to-perfection consistency elevate the experience to another level. The small dining room creates an intimate ambience that includes seating at the counter, right in the middle of the chefs at work.

3859 Piedmont Avenue
510-653-3902
commisrestaurant.com

KEEP IT CHILL
AT BAR 355

Bar 355 has a little something for everyone. Cheap cans of beer are sold alongside craft cocktails. Leather lounge seating invites patrons who want to chill, while others can dance on the small stage, usually adorned with glowing lights bouncing off the overhead disco ball. On weekend nights, rotating DJs spin classic vinyl, playing everything from Prince to Chaka Khan. Its long wooden bar and speakeasy setting simply make people feel relaxed, which is why it's become a hot spot for service industry folks and other professionals working downtown. The bar also gives back, occasionally hosting fund-raisers for nonprofit organizations, such as Planned Parenthood.

355 19th Street
510-451-3355

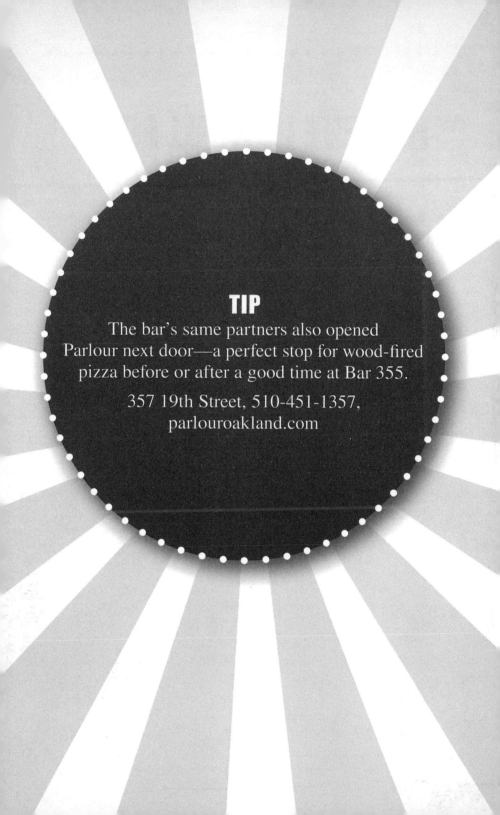

TIP

The bar's same partners also opened
Parlour next door—a perfect stop for wood-fired
pizza before or after a good time at Bar 355.

357 19th Street, 510-451-1357,
parlouroakland.com

BELIEVE IN SOUL FOOD
AT BROWN SUGAR KITCHEN

Yes, the fuss over Brown Sugar Kitchen is very real and very much put West Oakland on the map before opening its second location in Uptown. Chef Tanya Holland combines her former French training with her family's soul food history and—*voilà*—food magic happens. While the soul food classics on the menu (buttermilk fried chicken and BBQ shrimp and grits) are delish, the home-baked goods are equally melt-in-your-mouth good. The cornmeal waffle with brown sugar butter and apple cider syrup is a brunch must, while the beignets served with seasonal jam are a delicious order for the table. It's no wonder the restaurant has received so many accolades from near and far. Note: Like most Bay Area establishments with a reputation, the wait here can be fierce—but well worth it.

2534 Mandela Parkway
510-839-SOUL
and
2295 Broadway
brownsugarkitchen.com

TIP

Vegans can have their own soul food experience at Souley Vegan in Jack London Square. The restaurant's entirely vegan menu doesn't skimp on flavor either— so much so that it's hard to believe that the Creole pop'ens are made with vegan cheese.

301 Broadway, 510-922-1615, souleyvegan.com

EXPLORE THE MANY TASTES OF OAKLAND
AT SWAN'S MARKET

Swan's Market is perfect for groups of people who can't decide about where to eat. Its food court–style setup offers the convenience of picking and choosing from a variety of food outlets without skimping on quality. In fact, some of Oakland's most popular restaurants are located here—all of which offer the local, sustainable ingredients for which California cuisine is known. The Cook and Her Farmer serves up oysters from nearby Tomales Bay alongside kale and toasted quinoa salad. Equally fresh Cosecha Café features made-from-scratch tortillas, pastries, and traditional Mexican entrées, such as carne adovada. Or try the Afro-Caribbean cooking at Miss Ollie's, where the jerk shrimp are both big and spicy. After picking out your food choices, your group can all sit together at the wooden communal tables in the middle.

510 9th Street
510-287-5353
swansmarket.com

SHARE THE GARBAGE BREAD
AT PORTAL

Located a stone's throw from Lake Merritt on the south side, this restaurant is very unassuming from its exterior. Large trees, shrubbery, and a wooden fence hide its shining gem of a patio from lake goers, but locals know better than to pass it by. Upon entry, it feels like a very small restaurant, most of which is taken up by its bar, and it's not until you get to the deck out back that you see where the real party happens. Wooden communal tables (yes, they're everywhere in Oakland) line the deck where patrons are happily sipping beer, sharing plates of brewpub fare, and likely overhearing reggae music on the loudspeaker. The menu's highlight is the garbage bread, but don't let its name fool you. This delicious cheesy bread (which comes in both meat and vegetarian options) is anything but garbage, especially when combined with its pesto and marinara dipping sauces. The burger, beer selection, daily brunch menu, and bottomless mimosas on Saturdays and Sundays are also worth the quick trek south.

1611 2nd Avenue
510-663-7678
portaloakland.com

WAIT FOR THE MOUTHWATERING CHICKEN SANDWICH
AT BAKESALE BETTY

The line outside Bakesale Betty starts to form before the restaurant's 11:00 a.m. opening and continues to grow during the only three hours it stays open each day (Tuesdays through Saturdays). Everyone in line is there for one thing and one thing only: the buttermilk fried chicken and coleslaw sandwich (or the tofu version for vegetarians). The restaurant has a cult following so large that people drive from all over the Bay Area to get a taste of this delicious fried goodness that's piled high on a baguette. While there is only one sandwich on the menu, customers can also grab some of the restaurant's delicious baked goods—strawberry shortcakes, scones, and cookies—to top off the experience with something sweet.

5098 Telegraph Avenue
510-985-1213
bakesalebetty.com

TIP

If the line is too long at Bakesale Betty, head over to nearby Beauty's Bagel Shop. Known for its delicious wood-fired bagels (that even New Yorkers claim to be good), the shop offers a wide range of sandwiches, including an organic fried chicken sandwich with creamy beet coleslaw.

3838 Telegraph Avenue, 510-788-6098, beautysbagelshop.com

DROOL OVER DUMPLINGS
AT SHAN DONG RESTAURANT

A trip to the Bay Area would not be complete without a taste of dumplings, and Shan Dong does them just right. Located in the heart of Chinatown, the restaurant features a buzzing ambience typical of most Chinese restaurants in the area, but its pork dumplings are anything but ordinary. Crafted with a thick dough on the outside and a blend of pork and veggies on the inside, the dumplings essentially melt in your mouth. Also, make sure to order the restaurant's homemade chow mein noodles, which are hand pulled right in front of you as you wait for a table. The noodle soups are equally delicious if you order them with the same homemade noodles—thick and soft, the way nature intended.

328 10th Street
510-839-2299
sd.222.to

BREATHE IN THE DELICIOUS SMELLS
AT ARIZMENDI BAKERY

Arizmendi Bakery is one of six bakeries that make up the Arizmendi Association of Cooperatives, which are all worker-owned. As such, the employees here are truly passionate about serving up the artisan breads, morning pastries, and pizza made daily. Using only organic ingredients and creating only vegetarian pizzas, the bakery brings healthy options to all who enter. The pizza menu rotates daily, but the pizza is always crafted using thin organic sourdough crust and whole-milk mozzarella topped with seasonal vegetables. It's so good that customers never care what surprise toppings are in store for the day, and they can order pizza by the slice or half and whole pies.

3265 Lakeshore Avenue
510-268-8849
arizmendilakeshore.com

CALL IN SOME SUSHI
FROM GETA

Geta's tiny storefront location in Oakland's Piedmont neighborhood warrants a visit if you have a small party or want to grab a quick solo bite at the sushi bar. Its true calling, however, is takeout or delivery. The restaurant's affordable prices for quality sushi means it rarely gets a break from the steady stream of orders coming in. Customers can choose from the large menu of rolls that are all crafted to order. Its spider roll is deliciously crispy, while the fatty toro is so fresh that it's difficult to have just one. The menu even caters to those who haven't joined the sushi craze, with a large selection of teriyakis and tempuras.

165 41st Street
510-653-4643
getasushioakland.com

TIP

Another fun sushi spot to visit is Coach Sushi, where customers can order bottomless sake served in bamboo boxes for cheap as long as they spend a set price on food.

532 Grand Avenue, 510-834-7866, coachsushi.com

SIP YOUR WAY
ALONG THE OAKLAND
URBAN WINE TRAIL

A trip to the Bay Area wouldn't be complete without tasting some quality California wines, but not everyone has the time or money to make their way up to wine country. Luckily, Oakland has amped up its urban wine scene, with several urban wineries opening in renovated warehouses in Jack London Square and other parts of downtown. Founded in 2010, an association of ten wineries created the Oakland Urban Wine Trail for locals and visitors alike to taste their way through the city's top wineries—all of which are within walking distance. Sourcing their grapes from all over California, the wineries offer that same NorCal wine taste with the option to explore downtown Oakland in between stops.

oaklandurbanwinetrail.com

TIP

One of the best ways to explore the urban wine trail is through East Bay Winery Bike Tours, a full-day exploration of Oakland's wine scene with stops at three to four wineries and a picnic lunch.

724 Santa Ray Avenue, 510-285-7884, eastbaywinerybiketours.com

DEVOUR LATE-NIGHT MEXICAN FOOD
AT TACOS MI RANCHO

Mexican food is at its best in the Bay Area when served out of a taco truck or hole-in-the-wall taqueria. That's very much the case in Oakland, where both dot International Boulevard as you head south into Fruitvale. One of the area's most popular taco trucks is Tacos Mi Rancho, especially for its location near Lake Merritt. You can purchase $2 tacos and take them for a picnic alongside the lake. Customers choose from traditional Mexican meats, such as al pastor, carnitas, or even lengua (tongue), to customize other Mexican staples, ranging from tortas to the taco truck's famous 15-inch burrito. This truck caters especially to the late-night crowd, staying open until 3:00 a.m. on weekends. Note: The taco truck is cash only.

1434 1st Avenue
510-395-1403

SAVOR
HOUSE-ROASTED COFFEE
FROM TIMELESS COFFEE ROASTERS

All the coffee served at Timeless Coffee Roasters is roasted in-house, creating not only delicious coffee but also a delicious aroma every time you enter. The other highlight about this neighborhood coffee shop is that it doubles as a bakery, serving everything from cookies to cakes to truffles made by professional chocolatiers. The shop's waffle special served Monday through Friday from 7:00 a.m. to 10:30 a.m. really draws customers in for a morning treat, with different flavors rotating monthly. A cornmeal waffle with fresh berries is just one example. All of this is happening in an atmosphere so friendly that it seems staff members know almost everyone who walks inside. On sunny days, the café's bistro tables situated along the sidewalk in this quaint part of Piedmont give it a European vibe that is simply timeless.

4252 Piedmont Avenue
510-985-1360
timelesscoffee.com

TAKE PRIDE IN THE COUNTRY'S OLDEST LGBT BAR:
WHITE HORSE BAR

Operational since 1933 (or maybe even before, since records weren't kept during Prohibition), the White Horse Bar has seen the LGBT community through thick and thin as the oldest continuously operating gay and lesbian bar in the U.S. It has long served as a refuge for members of the LGBT community to be themselves, managing to not get raided during the '50s and '60s when patrons of gay bars across the country were being arrested for visiting similar establishments. Today, it still stands as a gay Cheers bar where most patrons know each other's names and a wide age range of LGBT community members call it home. DJs, karaoke nights, and drag shows keep it lively until 2:00 a.m. most nights of the week.

6551 Telegraph Avenue
510-652-3820
whitehorsebar.com

BEG FOR BACON
AT THE GASTROPIG

The Gastropig checks all the boxes you need in a quick, grab-and-go sandwich spot. Its central location in downtown makes it a top choice for business professionals, while its pork-centric menu makes it ideal for foodies in need of a good bacon fix. While its delicious Ode to Genova ham sandwich or seasonal salads cater to the lunch crowd, this spot's true calling is breakfast sandwiches. In particular, its Baconslut sandwich—made with Applewood smoked bacon, an over-easy egg, sharp cheddar cheese, and smokey Aleppo aioli atop a brioche roll—brings everything that is good about breakfast into one ultimate bite. Other standouts include the Not Your Momma's PB&J with chunky peanut butter and seasonal jam on a croissant or its Waffle Iron Hashbrown with cheddar and scallions.

2123 Franklin Street
510-817-4663
thegastropig.com

MUSIC AND ENTERTAINMENT

GET INTO A GROOVE
AT THE FOX OAKLAND

A trip to Oakland wouldn't be complete without a visit to the Fox. Originally built in 1928 and listed on the National Register of Historic Places, this historic theater is one of downtown's shining gems, with a sign out front that literally lights up the streets any night a show is playing. The former movie house turned music venue reopened its doors in February 2009 after a $75 million renovation that managed to maintain some of its best Middle Eastern architectural elements, including two golden statues located on each side of the stage. Popular artists—Paul Simon, Widespread Panic, Metallica, and Van Morrison to name just a few—have graced the stage, while President Barack Obama even spoke here during his 2012 campaign. Before a show, ticket holders can grab a drink at the downstairs bar, cleverly dubbed the Den. For the ultimate experience, though, you can upgrade to get VIP access to the Telegraph Room, with a private bar, complimentary appetizers, and entry to a preferred viewing section on the venue's orchestra level.

1807 Telegraph Avenue
510-302-2250
thefoxoakland.com

COMPETE FOR TICKETS TO BRUNO MARS (OR THE LIKE)
AT ORACLE ARENA

Located adjacent to Oakland-Alameda Coliseum, Oracle Arena is the indoor arena yin to the Coliseum's outdoor stadium yang. Home to the Golden State Warriors (for now until they make the infamous move across the Bay), Oracle Arena is the spot in Oakland to attract top-name acts, such as Bruno Mars; Earth, Wind & Fire; and Stevie Nicks. While there's no better way to experience a concert than from the floor level, the arena's luxury suites are a close second. Personalized service, access to private restrooms, and in-suite foods to nosh on are major perks, and the views from this level are hard to beat. Plus, you have a lot of space to test out your best dance moves with your favorite music fans. Note: Search for tickets the second they go on sale because top-act shows here sell out fast.

7000 Coliseum Way
510-569-2121
oracleareana.com

UNITE WITH LOCAL ARTISTS
AT STORK CLUB

This divey music venue has been around for years and never seems to disappoint no matter how random the entertainment. Almost every night of the week, some sort of local music or theatrical performance is here to check out. Coinciding with Oakland First Fridays, the venue hosts its First Friday Follies to entertain the masses that spill in from Telegraph Avenue. This free burlesque show is so popular that patrons often arrive early for a spot, even if the best you can find is a seat on the floor. On other nights, you can experience such events as Open Bluegrass on Mondays, when a group of local bluegrass musicians gather in a circle to jam out on fiddles, acoustic guitars, and banjos. Techno Tuesdays is equally entertaining.

2330 Telegraph Avenue
510-444-6174
storkcluboakland.com

DANCE YOUR BOOTY OFF
AT BISSAP BAOBAB

Part Senegalese restaurant, part late-night dance club, this place brings a taste of Africa to Oakland. Fish dinners served with couscous or rice, topped off with a hibiscus-infused cocktail are an ideal way to start the night, but the spot is really famous for its dancing. Live bands or DJs pump up the jams into the wee hours, with Latin salsa dancing and Afrofunk that offer rhythmic beats. The dancing here is some of the best (and sweatiest) in the Bay Area, so prepare to bust out some moves. The restaurant has been at the heart of the Bay Area community since opening its original location in San Francisco's Mission District in 1996. While food and dancing are key to the venue's festivities, it also serves as a haven for West Africans looking to speak French, watch the World Cup, listen to poetry, and simply embrace their heritage.

381 15th Street
510-817-4722
bissapbaobab.com

LISTEN TO JAZZ
AT YOSHI'S JAZZ CLUB

Yoshi's has everything you want in a quality jazz club. What started as a simple Berkeley sushi bar in the 1970s turned into one of the Bay Area's most respected venues to see jazz. Booked basically every night of the week, Yoshi's 310-seat space in Jack London Square has hosted such musical acts as Tower of Power, Taj Mahal, and Talib Kweli. These popular performances often have two shows in one night because the club wants to continue its intimate seating format, placing patrons around tables so that they can enjoy the music while comfortably drinking a cocktail. The spot's sushi origin isn't lost, either, as anyone can enjoy dinner in the dining room before making their way into the theater space. Just be sure to make a reservation beforehand.

510 Embarcadero West
510-238-9200
yoshis.com

REVISIT HOLLYWOOD'S GOLDEN ERA
AT THE PARAMOUNT THEATRE

Built in 1931, this Art Deco movie theater was once the largest multipurpose theater on the West Coast, seating 3,476. Giving the Fox a run for its money, the Paramount's exterior also touts an impressive sign that beckons passersby when lit up on performance nights. Its interior, however, is what makes going to a show here unforgettable. Gold dancing figures and green artificial light panels illuminate the lobby space, screaming of Hollywood's Golden Era, while vintage telephones pay homage to the past. Even what appear to be the original water fountains are still in use. Venture farther inside and the theater space is equally as decadent with a gold ceiling grid. While the space itself is reason enough to go, the theater also attracts some of the best acts in town. In between hosting the Oakland Symphony and Oakland Ballet, acts ranging from Prince to Jerry Seinfeld have graced the stage with their presence.

2025 Broadway
510-465-6400
paramounttheatre.com

SEE A MOVIE
AT GRAND LAKE THEATRE

Yet another area vintage theater is the Grand Lake Theatre, which was built in 1926. This one, however, still operates as a movie palace. On Friday and Saturday evenings, the theater even still plays its Mighty Wurlitzer organ briefly before screenings. Unlike big-name movie conglomerates, movie tickets come at bargain prices by today's standards, especially with all-day discount tickets on Discount Tuesdays. The theater has several auditoriums—each with its own theme—but the main theater is definitely its shining gem, featuring intricate gold furnishings and curtains. While the design is vintage, the theater still keeps up with the times, offering 3D movies and even hosting community film festivals of all kinds. (Past ones have included the popular and very Bay Area BRIEFS Erotic Short Film Competition.)

3200 Grand Avenue
510-452-3556
renaissancerialto.com

DRESS UP FOR A NIGHT
WITH THE OAKLAND SYMPHONY

Going to the symphony is still alive and well in Oakland. The Oakland Symphony, Oakland Symphony Chorus, and Oakland Symphony Youth Orchestra combine to form a single nonprofit organization geared toward making classical and symphonic music accessible to the Oakland community. Its "everyone is welcome" philosophy attracts a wide range of patrons, from college students dressed in jeans to grandparents who have had season tickets for years. At the symphony's helm, Maestro Michael Morgan has led it for more than twenty-five years now and presents a wide range of programs that appeal to the East Bay's culturally diverse market. During the summer, the Symphony Chorus even hosts a Summer Sing-Ins series for anyone in the public who wants to buy a ticket and sing along with the chorus. Most of the organization's performances are held at the area's historic Paramount Theatre.

2025 Broadway
(This is the Paramount Theatre,
but the organization's office is located elsewhere.)
510-444-0801
oaklandsymphony.org

SING POPULAR KARAOKE TUNES
AT THE ALLEY

About forty thousand to fifty thousand business cards—even ones from Greg Allman and California Governor Jerry Brown—line the walls and ceiling as a testament to the popularity and timelessness of this piano bar. On any given night, you will find patrons passing along a book of songs in the circle that automatically forms around the longtime pianist playing at the piano. They take turns holding the mic to sing classic karaoke hits out of the "Great American Songbook." The bar's laidback environment and no-stage performance space make it easy for even the not-so-outgoing visitor to belt out a song or two. Whether or not you decide to perform, the live piano and jolly-good customers make you even *want* to hear Elton John's "Tiny Dancer" or Billy Joel's "Piano Man" for the umpteenth time.

3325 Grand Avenue
510-444-8505

VISIT THE LEGIONNAIRE SALOON
FOR A LITTLE BIT OF EVERYTHING

With its distinct location on Telegraph Avenue, the Legionnaire Saloon caters to a wide audience who want to be part of the local music scene or to simply hang out. Local DJs provide a funky sound track to the scene downstairs, where arcade games entertain gamers in the back, TVs always play sports games for die-hard fans, and the Powers Irish Whiskey shot and pint o' Guinness beer special appeases the locals in need of a go-to watering hole. Upstairs, a stage awaits local performers playing to music aficionados in search of a new sound. Add to that a Sunday Beat-the-Clock event when all tap beers are only $1 starting at 8:00 p.m., with prices going up every thirty minutes until 10:30 p.m. If you're lucky, you'll also find a pop-up food option, with past examples including grilled steak tacos. Whatever the occasion, this spot has just about everything you could want in a music venue, watering hole, gaming spot, or whatever you want to call it—day and night.

2272 Telegraph Avenue
510-891-8660
legionnairesaloon.com

FIND UNEXPECTED ENTERTAINMENT
AT STARLINE SOCIAL CLUB

From the street, Starline Social Club looks like your typical trendy Oakland bar. Plants in the windows create an au naturel California ambience, and candles set the mood for intimate conversations. No one would expect that upstairs a hip-hop concert is going on or a yoga class—but that is very likely to be the case. The Starline Social Club has a packed calendar of events, with several happening each night, in both the Starline Ballroom upstairs and the restaurant and bar on the main level. Even its recurring events are way more exciting that your average trivia night. Showga on Wednesdays combines yoga instruction with live musical performances, while patrons can also enjoy Wake the Town Wednesdays with DJs spinning records downstairs. The restaurant, open for breakfast, lunch, and dinner, also attracts a daytime crowd, especially when invited chefs showcase their cuisine as part of a pop-up restaurant experience every Monday.

2236 Martin Luther King Junior Way
510-593-2109
starlinesocialclub.com

PICK A COUCH
AT NEW PARKWAY THEATER

Cozy couches and living room furniture very literally make a movie at New Parkway Theater comparable to watching a big-screen flick in the comfort of your own living room. The community-centric theater plays a combination of new hits and cult classics on any given day. But that's not all. Its free evening activities—Open Mic Monday, Bingo and Beer Tuesday, and Wednesday Art Night to name a few—always draw a crowd. Even if you're not up for a movie or an event, the theater has a collection of board games for anyone to play in the mezzanine while simultaneously chowing down on a slice of pizza or a sandwich from the theater's café. The best thing about this place is that you can take beer or wine into the theater for the ultimate date night at the cinema.

474 24th Street
510-658-7900
thenewparkway.com

CATCH SOME
LOCAL MUSIC
AT THE NEW PARISH

If you want to get a true taste of the local music scene, the New Parish is always a good time, especially if you're interested in soul, funk, and reggae beats. The independent music venue has a rotating calendar of local bands and DJs for affordable prices, but top acts, such as Ozomatli, Shuggie Otus, and Robert Randolph, have also been rotated into the calendar. The venue also hosts monthly events, such as thePeople, an event that brings together local artists of all kinds—musicians, painters, and even local chefs—shining a light on Oakland's creative community. Its expansive outdoor patio is also a choice spot to meet people in between sets.

1743 San Pablo Avenue
510-444-7474
thenewparish.com

SHAKE YOUR TAIL FEATHER
AT SOMAR BAR AND LOUNGE

Looking for some quality late-night dancing? Then Somar's the place to go. Located in the heart of downtown on Telegraph Avenue, this spot attracts a diverse crowd in search of some stellar nightlife. While its artwork-lined brick walls create an artsy lounge atmosphere, don't let them fool you. DJs often spin classic hip-hop and reggae until 2:00 a.m., making it a popular spot for anyone looking to dance the night away, especially after a concert at the Fox Oakland (a mere block away). Like several Oakland establishments, it, too, has a strong voice in the community, hosting happy hour fund-raisers for local organizations.

1727 Telegraph Avenue
somarbar.com/index.html

GIDDY UP FOR LINE DANCING
AT OVERLAND COUNTRY BAR & GRILL

The Wild West is alive and well at Overland Country Bar & Grill. Not only does its menu feature such typical Southwestern fare as chili verde, but live bluegrass, folk, or country music is also mixed in with country karaoke several nights of the week. The honky tonk scene made up of a wooden bar and wooden floors sets the stage for some foot-stompin' line dancing or two-stepping. With comfy booths and flatscreen TVs, it's also an ideal place to watch sports games, especially during the hours brunch is being served. You simply can't go wrong with the 1874 beef short rib hash.

101 Broadway
510-419-0594
overlandoakland.com

SEE AN OUTDOOR MUSICAL
AT WOODMINSTER AMPHITHEATER

Nothing says summer in Oakland quite like seeing an outdoor musical at Woodminster Amphitheater. Located in Joaquin Miller Park in the Oakland Hills, patrons can sing along to a combination of new and classic musicals, such as past renditions of "Mamma Mia!" or "South Pacific." The amphitheater has hosted under-the-star musicals since 1967, typically presenting three musicals a summer, with seven regular performances of each. While the shows are entertaining, the setting is equally worth a visit. The park's towering redwood trees surround the amphitheater, complete with standard seating. Even better, most patrons bring a picnic before the evening show, as there are no restrictions on bringing food or beverages into the theater.

3300 Joaquin Miller Road
510-531-9597
woodminster.com

CHECK OUT STAND-UP COMEDY & MORE
AT THE UPTOWN

Yet another live event venue in downtown, the Uptown offers a little something for everyone in that it has a large bar in one room, a small performance venue in another, and a smoking patio in back. Live music most nights of the week make it another choice spot to explore the local music scene for super reasonable rates. Free stand-up comedy nights on Wednesdays also give customers a reason to venture in on a weeknight. It's the ideal spot to see local comedy talent or test out some of your own comedy routines. The Uptown's drink selection is equally noteworthy, featuring an extensive list of cocktails and local beers.

1928 Telegraph Avenue
510-272-9446
uptownnightclub.com

STEP UP
YOUR SALSA GAME
AT CAÑA CUBAN PARLOR & CAFÉ

To be clear, Caña Cuban Parlor & Café is very much a restaurant, particularly known for its brunch. Delicious Cuban flavors redefine brunch classics, such as the chicken and waffles made with Cuban fried chicken, sweet potato waffles, and mango salsa. Or you can try the Machacha Cubano with slow-roasted, Cuban-style shredded pork, cacao black beans, sofrito, and verde sauce. On Sundays, though, this spot is widely known for its live salsa music and dancing from 3:00 p.m. to close. While the vibe is laidback and open for salsa newbies to test their dancing skills, make sure to step aside and let the regulars show off some of the best dancing techniques in the city. Note: The restaurant's bottomless mimosas definitely provide liquid courage for the dance floor.

530 Lake Park Avenue
510-832-1515
canaoakland.com

SPORTS AND RECREATION

BASK IN THE SUN
AT LAKE MERRITT

Lake Merritt and its surrounding green spaces (such as Lakeside Park) stands as Oakland's 155-acre focal point. It is both a fresh and saltwater lake with a 3.4-mile circumference that not only has paths for people to walk and bike around but also several green spaces that welcome picnics and cookouts on any given day. This outdoor haven, located just blocks from downtown, is home to the oldest designated wildlife refuge in the country, with several artificial bird islands that attract hundreds of egrets, herons, geese, and other types of birds. Even at night the lake greets visitors with a "necklace of lights" made of 3,400 pearly bulbs strung between 126 lampposts to help illuminate the space. Visitors can also get out on the lake by visiting Lake Merritt Boating Center, which rents out everything from pedal boats to kayaks to sailboats.

568 Bellevue Avenue
510-238-3187
lakemerritt.org

WITNESS STORIES COME TO LIFE
AT CHILDREN'S FAIRYLAND

Almost every local has fond childhood memories of Children's Fairyland. Located within Lakeside Park (situated along Lake Merritt), the ten-acre park was built in 1950 as the first "themed" amusement park in the U.S. and the first one created specifically for families with young children. It is even said to have inspired Walt Disney's vision for Disneyland. With about sixty storybook sets, the park brings childhood stories to life in such attractions as the Old Lady in the Shoe or the Alice in Wonderland tunnel. Visitors can also catch one of the three puppet performances a day at Fairyland's Storybook Puppet Theater, the oldest continuously operating puppet theater in the country. Note: The park only admits adults who are accompanied by children and vice versa.

699 Bellevue Avenue
510-452-2259
fairyland.org

WATCH A GAME
AT THE COLISEUM

Sports enthusiasts won't want to miss a game at the Oakland-Alameda County Coliseum—Coliseum for short—because Oakland has truly die-hard fans. Home to both the Raiders football and Oakland Athletics baseball franchises (until their possible big moves), the stadium offers the opportunity to watch sports during almost any given month of the year. Even though the teams have gone in and out of winning streaks through the decades, their fans remain extremely loyal and are more than ready to tailgate before a game. When the stadium's not hosting sports, it's been known to host large-scale concerts and events, such as Fleetwood Mac and the Rolling Stones. Located adjacent to Oracle Arena, the Coliseum does offer parking for visitors willing to wait in the infamous Bay Area traffic, but the stadium's stop on the BART line makes it an easy place to reach using public transportation.

7000 Coliseum Way
510-569-2121
coliseum.com

TAKE A STROLL THROUGH
MOUNTAIN VIEW CEMETERY

An unexpected Oakland hangout is Mountain View Cemetery, located in the hills of Oakland and Piedmont. This 226-acre cemetery touts some of the best views in the entire Bay Area not to mention some of the area's best landscaping. Designed by Frederick Law Olmsted, the landscape architect who designed New York City's Central Park, the park features several fountains matched by massive mausoleums that hold some of the area's wealthiest historical figures, including railroad magnate Charles Crocker and architect Julia Morgan. The setting is so picturesque that you will find several visitors on any given day. Some are here to jog amidst the native oak trees, while others are here to picnic beside their loved one's graves. The combination of nature and humanity creates a spiritual sense that nearly takes your breath away.

5000 Piedmont Avenue
510-658-2588
mountainviewcemetery.org

PARTY A LA BIKE
AT THE EAST BAY BIKE PARTY

Nothing says an Oakland party like one with bikes. Almost every artsy hipster in the East Bay owns and rides a bike, and now the trend is spreading like wildfire. Case in point: Every second Friday of the month, bike enthusiasts gather to celebrate community in this ultimate mobile party. The ten- to fifteen-mile route changes monthly, but it always meets near a BART station to encourage public transit use and a car-free event. The year-round event meets at 7:30 p.m. and encourages everyone to start riding by 8:00 p.m. While the ride may seem serious, it's not. Each month since its May 2010 inception, the event has a different theme for people to dress up and accessorize in true Bay Area form—not to mention the music blaring as you ride.

eastbaybikeparty.wordpress.com

EXPLORE NORCAL'S FAMOUS REDWOODS
AT REDWOOD REGIONAL PARK

Forget making the trek to Marin County to see Muir Woods or driving five hours north to visit Redwood National and State Parks. There's a hidden 1,830-acre redwood forest located in the Oakland Hills that's just as peaceful as the more famous ones. Visitors can hike amid the towering 150-foot coast redwoods *(Sequoia sempervirens)* and catch sight of deer, raccoons, rabbits, and, if you're lucky, a golden eagle. Dogs are allowed, but technically they require a small fee collected at the Redwood Gate entrance. Same goes for parking; however, there's street parking that's free. Note: No matter how warm it is outside, pack a sweater. The density of the trees allows for little sunlight to shine through, creating a cool environment that can be chilly if you're not moving fast enough.

7867 Redwood Road
888-327-2757
ebparks.org/parks/redwood

VENTURE AROUND LUSH CREEKS
AT JOAQUIN MILLER PARK

Owned and operated by the city of Oakland, this park offers a similar sense of solitude as the neighboring Redwood Regional Park to the east and features the same coast redwood trees as its counterpart. This slightly smaller five-hundred-acre park is ideal for hikers, bicyclists, joggers, and picnickers alike, and also allows dogs as long as they're on a leash. Locals enjoy walking the variety of terrain as they hike the hilly woodland trails through redwood groves and oak tree forests across lush creeks and through vast meadows. A visit to the Joaquin Miller Park Ranger Station can be fun to see the current wildlife exhibit on display or to gather more information about the park's history—named after famous poet Joaquin Miller. Park facilities are also available for picnics or even larger gatherings, such as family reunions or weddings.

3300 Joaquin Miller Road
510-238-7275
oaklandnet.com

KAYAK THE OAKLAND ESTUARY
WITH CALIFORNIA CANOE & KAYAK

The Oakland Estuary, the strait that separates Oakland from Alameda and connects to both San Francisco Bay and San Leandro Bay, is an ideal place to practice some kayaking or stand up paddle boarding. California Canoe & Kayak provides kayak rentals directly out of Jack London Square for urban kayaking at its finest. As you make your way past the eateries along the water, heading south toward San Leandro, the surroundings become much more serene. Seals, leopard sharks, and bat rays can be spotted, while birds fly overhead. For beginners, California Canoe & Kayak offers daylong kayaking and stand up paddle board classes that include gear and instructions on how to paddle safely.

409 Water Street
510-893-7833
calkayak.com

TAKE A DIP OR TWO
AT PIEDMONT SPRINGS

While Oakland offers many places to relax, nothing quite competes with Piedmont Springs. The spa offers the typical massages and skin care treatments, while its four private, outdoor hot tubs provide an idyllic way to get some R&R without a hefty price tag. You can spend an hour soaking up the 102° Fahrenheit warmth on a foggy Oakland day. Or book the hot tub at night and catch a glimpse of the stars on a clear evening. Better yet, reserve the Combination Room and spend your time going back and forth between hot tub and sauna. The hot tubs and surrounding walls are completely made of redwood that takes you to a cabin retreat far from the city—even if just for an hour.

3939 Piedmont Avenue
510-652-9191
piedmontsprings.com

CHOOSE BETWEEN BOWLING OR ARCADE GAMES
AT PLANK

Located in the heart of Jack London Square is Plank, a high-end, indoor/outdoor entertainment center geared to engage the child in everyone. First, you have eighteen lanes of bowling inside with three massive screens over the pins for bowlers to watch sports or the like. Across the way, a wide range of patrons can play arcade games that range from skeet ball to air hockey. The beer garden out back completes the entertainment offerings with bocce ball courts and cornhole board sets. Of course, Plank's more than fifty local beers attract the drinking crowd as well, and the food goes beyond your typical bowling alley fare, featuring smoked pork belly tacos and baby kale salad.

98 Broadway
510-817-0980
plankoakland.com

JOIN THE CIRCUS
AT TRAPEZE ARTS

Whether you want to join the circus for a day or permanently, Trapeze Arts has you covered. As one of only a few full-time circus schools in the US, Trapeze Arts offers flying trapeze and circus arts classes in ten thousand square feet of well-padded space, which is where the magic happens, with a wide assortment of professionals and novices, both young and old, practicing flying trapeze tricks, trampoline jumps, tight-wire rope balancing, and all kinds of juggling skills. Classes are available most days of the week, so both locals and visitors can partake and learn how to glide through the air in no time.

1822 9th Street
510-410-0700
trapezearts.com

SEARCH FOR A LABYRINTH
AT SIBLEY VOLCANIC REGIONAL PRESERVE

Yes, up in the hills surrounding Oakland there was once a volcano that makes up present-day Sibley Volcanic Regional Preserve. Round Top, one of the preserve's highest peaks at an elevation of 1,763 feet, is made up of lava and volcanic debris from the ten million-year-old volcano. Several trails take visitors all over the preserve, but it's the thirty-one-mile East Bay Skyline National Recreation Trail that connects the preserve to other regional parks, such as Wildcat Canyon to the north and Anthony Chabot to the south. This park is especially popular for its labyrinths—yes, plural—the largest of which is visible from the peak and was created by East Bay resident Helena Mazzariello. Most trails are for hiking and equestrian use only, but some also allow bicycles.

6701 Skyline Boulevard
888-327-2757
ebparks.org/parks/sibley

WAVE TO A MONKEY
AT OAKLAND ZOO

Animal lovers will want to make their way to the southeast side of town to visit the Oakland Zoo. This playful animal kingdom has been a staple in the Oakland community since 1922 and continues to remain fresh for new generations of zoo goers as it transitions from the traditional zoo concept into more of a wild animal park. In June 2017, it opened a gondola ride that takes families above the Oakland Hills to a restaurant with views. These changes are just the beginning of the zoo's California Trail expansion (to be completed summer 2018) that adds fifty-five acres of land and eight native-to-California animals, such as grizzly bears, American bison, and mountain lions. Visitors can still see the same chimpanzees and tigers in the Tropical Rainforest exhibit or giraffes in the African Veldt exhibit. They will now see them through a newer lens.

9777 Golf Links Road
510-632-9525
oaklandzoo.org

PRACTICE YOUR GOLF SWING
AT MONTCLAIR GOLF CLUB

This nine-hole pitch-and-putt course offers a no-frills vibe that makes it the perfect place for children, beginning golfers, or those who simply have only a couple of hours to practice their golf swings. What really makes it stand out is its two-story driving range where golfers can practice hitting balls into a valley of trees. The best part: You can order a beer from the club's bar and take it to the range. The restaurant also serves up some delicious bar and grill fare that continue the all-American feel that this place ever-so-coolly exudes. Because not many people seem to know about Montclair Golf Club, it also has less of a crowd than many other Oakland establishments.

2477 Monterey Boulevard
510-482-0422

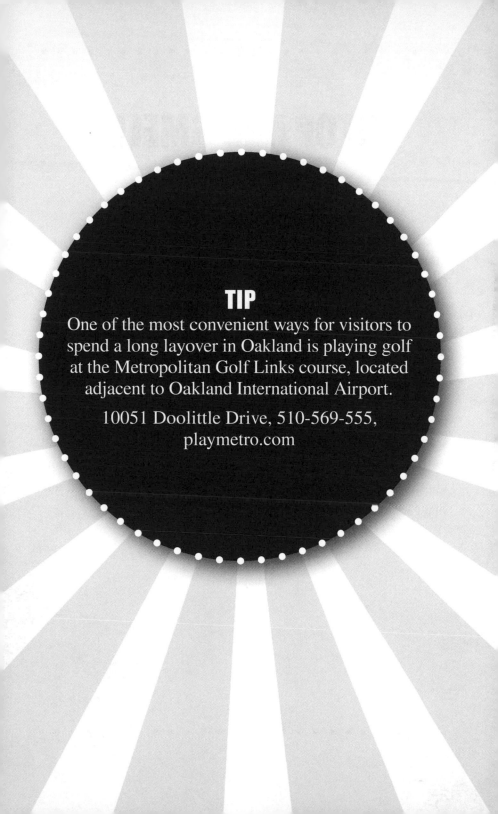

TIP

One of the most convenient ways for visitors to spend a long layover in Oakland is playing golf at the Metropolitan Golf Links course, located adjacent to Oakland International Airport.

10051 Doolittle Drive, 510-569-555,
playmetro.com

STOP AND SMELL THE ROSES
IN MORCOM ROSE GARDEN

Summer is the best time of year to visit the Morcom Rose Garden, but it really provides an escape any time of year, with roses usually staying in bloom as late as the end of October. Its location in the middle of a residential part of Piedmont makes it almost a secret—something that visitors have to seek out instead of the other way around. The garden's thousands of roses wind in and out of walkways, a reflecting pool, and cascading fountain, making it an ideal date spot or family outing. Constructed in 1932, it has stood the test of time as a place for weddings, receptions, and memorials. Free guided walking tours are available twice weekly, highlighting the city's skyline and other landmarks in the area.

700 Jean Street
510-238-3187
oaklandnet.com

SLIDE ACROSS THE ICE
AT OAKLAND ICE CENTER

Oakland's temperate climate makes it difficult to find any real winter activities to explore, but Oakland Ice Center is the exception, offering public skate sessions at reasonable rates on any given day. There's also drop-in ice hockey available as well as unstructured hockey time that the rink playfully dubs "Gretzky Hour." (Full ice hockey gear is required for both.) Of course, locals can sign up for figure skating classes and youth or adult hockey leagues, and real ice skating diehards can join Coffee Club, a twice weekly adults-only session for open skating practice, complete with a cup of coffee and pastry.

519 18th Street
510-268-9000
oaklandice.com

RIDE A FERRY
FROM JACK LONDON SQUARE

There's nothing more Bay Area than taking a ferry across the San Francisco Bay, especially on a sunny day when the Bay Bridge and Golden Gate Bridge are lit up in all their glory. You can catch several ferries from Oakland's Jack London Square Terminal to several terminals in San Francisco using San Francisco Bay Ferry's daily service. That includes the San Francisco Ferry Building, where ferry goers can step off to explore the city, or further their adventure by riding the Golden Gate Ferry to other Bay Area stops, such as Sausalito or Tiburon. Whether it's sunny outside or not, don't forget to bring a jacket on the ride because the wind can get quite chilly out on the water.

10 Clay Street
707-64-FERRY
sanfranciscobayferry.com

JUMP INTO THE BAY
AT CROWN MEMORIAL STATE BEACH

While this beach is technically in the city of Alameda (a mere fifteen-minute drive from downtown Oakland), it had to be mentioned because it's hands down the best beach experience in the East Bay. A couple of miles of beach line the San Francisco Bay with beautiful views of San Francisco in the distance. It's an ideal spot to catch some rays or picnic with family and friends, and on a hot sunny day, the water feels extra refreshing. Because the waves aren't as massive as the ones rolling into San Francisco's Ocean Beach, it's also the perfect spot to learn how to windsurf. Conveniently enough, Boardsports California has a beachfront location, with equipment and lessons available.

8th Street and Otis Drive
888-327-2757
ebparks.org/parks/crown_beach

CULTURE AND HISTORY

EXPERIENCE THE ULTIMATE BLOCK PARTY
AT OAKLAND FIRST FRIDAYS

What started in 2006 as a single-block art gallery walk known as the 23rd Street Fair has since grown into the ultimate block party spanning five blocks on Telegraph Avenue (from Grand Avenue to 27th Street). As its name implies, every first Friday of the month local artists, musicians, dancers, and roughly thirty thousand patrons gather to celebrate the Oakland community. That includes vendors selling jewelry and artwork, a couple of temporary stages for musicians and a plethora of food trucks. The festivities start at 5:00 p.m. and don't end until 9:30 p.m., but the sooner you go, the better selection of artisan goods you'll see. Note: The original art galleries that are now part of the Oakland Art Murmur collective still open their galleries to the public during First Fridays, but they evolved into a separate entity in 2012.

oaklandfirstfridays.org

PERUSE ARTWORK
DURING THE OAKLAND ART MURMUR SATURDAY STROLL

Now that Oakland First Fridays has become so massive, the Oakland Art Murmur (OAM) hosts a Saturday Stroll to provide a quieter and more focused way for visitors to view art at the more than fifty OAM galleries. The event is different from the collective's First Friday event in that the Saturday Stroll is available to the public every Saturday from 1:00 p.m. to 5:00 p.m. This is also when many of the galleries host free artist talks, receptions, film screenings, and trunk shows to promote the visual arts in the Oakland community. Lucky patrons who are available on the third Saturday of the month from 2:00 p.m. to 4:00 p.m. can also take the free Gallery District Walking Tour to learn more about the member galleries and current exhibits.

oaklandartmurmur.org

INTERACT WITH HISTORY
AT OAKLAND MUSEUM OF CALIFORNIA

Opened in 1969, Oakland Museum of California (OMCA) is an unexpected treasure in the heart of downtown. While it focuses on the city's culture and history, it also pays homage to the entire state of California across its three gallery spaces: Natural Sciences on Level 1, History on Level 2, and Art on Level 3. Its History level, for instance, takes visitors on an exploration of the Wild West and 1920s Hollywood through the Summer of Love and the beginning of tech culture. What really makes the museum stand out, though, is its Brutalist architecture that mixes concrete with a variety of outdoor elements on all three levels. A fan favorite is the Oak Street Plaza, which includes scattered chairs and tables alongside a giant chalk board for anyone to use. Every week the museum hosts its Friday Nights at OMCA with food trucks and live music, and gallery admissions are half off for adults and free for anyone under eighteen. Note: The museum is closed Monday and Tuesday.

1000 Oak Street
510-318-8400
museumca.org

STARGAZE
AT THE CHABOT SPACE AND SCIENCE CENTER

Science and astronomy lovers go crazy over this place that especially caters to children. While its planetarium alone is worth the trip, it also features special exhibits based on work supported by different earth and space programs. Its Touch the Sun exhibit lets visitors play with plasma and sculpt sunspots using powerful magnets. Or the One Giant Leap: A Moon Odyssey exhibit puts visitors behind the controls of a Mercury space capsule and also features a moon rock from the Apollo 15 mission. Night Hikes through the nearby redwoods and various laser and planetarium shows mix well with the hands-on activities and demonstrations going on throughout the center. The center's $5 First Fridays gives visitors on a budget the option to experience the science center at night from 6:00 to 10:00. Note: The science center stays open late on Fridays and Saturdays for telescope viewings during the summer months and is closed Mondays and Tuesdays.

10000 Skyline Boulevard
510-336-7373
chabotspace.org

WALK THE GROUNDS
OF OAKLAND CALIFORNIA TEMPLE

The thirteenth operating temple in existence for The Church of Jesus Christ of Latter-day Saints (the Mormon Church) resides in the Oakland Hills overlooking the San Francisco Bay. While, yes, it offers another magnificent view of the area, its architecture also gives it historic significance in the community. More than fifty years old, the 170-foot high temple's five-spire design creates a castle-like grandiose structure that seems massive when you stand at its foot. Its landscaping provides a tranquil setting, as flowers and palm trees line the man-made creek running from one fountain to another. Free tours of the grounds are available from the visitors center daily. Note: The temple is undergoing a massive renovation in 2018 to bring it up to code.

4770 Lincoln Avenue
510-531-3200
ldschurchtemples.com/oakland

SOAK IN THE CHARM
THAT IS PRESERVATION PARK

Preservation Park highlights the Oakland of the past. The historic Victorian houses that line the streets of the two-block neighborhood date back to the 1870s. Lush gardens, traditional park benches, old-fashioned street lamps, wrought-iron fences, and a Parisian fountain complement the sixteen buildings that have been preserved to now serve as event spaces and offices for nonprofit organizations and small businesses that further the Oakland community. Only five of the homes are native to the site, while eleven were relocated from their original locations south of 13th Street to avoid demolition. The park is open to the public during the day to tour and reminisce about the city's history.

1233 Preservation Park Way
510-874-7580
preservationpark.com

PLAY WITH FIRE
AT THE CRUCIBLE

The Crucible is a dream world for those who love to get crafty with fire. This nonprofit arts education organization caters to the industrial arts, offering a hands-on environment for community members to learn a variety of skill sets, from welding to glass blowing to woodworking to jewelry making to even fire dancing. With more than 175 classes and workshops, the Crucible offers classes designed for beginners, experienced tradespeople, and everyone in between to get behind a flame if they so desire. It also hosts events—Fire Arts Festivals, fire operas, and the annual Hot Couture fashion show—to allow community members to show off their skills. Even if you don't have time to take a class, the Crucible offers free guided tours of its 56,000-square-foot facility twice a month: every first Tuesday at 6:00 p.m. and every third Saturday at 3:00 p.m. (except during holidays and special events). Note: Locals can rent out studio space to get more involved in the creative community.

1260 7th Street
510-444-0919
thecrucible.org

STEP ABOARD
FDR'S "FLOATING WHITE HOUSE" KNOWN AS THE USS *POTOMAC*

Originally built as the U.S. Coast Guard Cutter *Electra* in 1934, the "Floating White House" was later commissioned as a U.S. Navy vessel in 1936, renamed the USS *Potomac* and served as Franklin Delano Roosevelt's presidential yacht until he died in 1945. The 165-foot vessel even played a role during his presidency when Roosevelt organized a secret conference to develop the Atlantic Charter. As one of two presidential yachts still in existence, she is now preserved in Oakland's Jack London Square and considered a National Historic Landmark. Dockside tours on most Wednesdays, Fridays, and Saturdays provide an hour-long history of the *Potomac*, while three-hour public cruises on San Francisco Bay are also available from June through Veterans Day. Stepping aboard the public cruise, guests will visit surrounding landmarks and learn about the history of the effects that FDR's administration had on the Bay Area.

540 Water Street
510-627-1215
usspotomac.org

GET CRAFTY
AT MUSEUM OF CHILDREN'S ARTS (MOCHA)

If your children love art, Museum of Children's Arts (MOCHA) is the place for them. Founded in 1989, MOCHA started with artist residency programs, partnering with local schools and bringing children's art exhibits to community sites, such as hospitals and city buildings. Now, its downtown museum offers several interactive exhibits and art programs, which are ideal for school field trips and art parties. Art lessons can range from mask design to clay exploration to painting pictures of animals. The museum's Open Studio drop-in program is available on a first-come, first-served basis. Children can make their way through the museum's six different areas, including the Imagine Lab and Great Wall of Paint, to participate in hands-on art activities.

1625 Clay Street
510-465-8770
mocha.org

DELVE INTO HISTORY
WITH THE AFRICAN AMERICAN
MUSEUM & LIBRARY AT OAKLAND

While the entire Oakland Public Library system offers an extensive network of resources, the noncirculating African American Museum Library at Oakland brings the community more than 160 collections on the history of African Americans in Northern California and the Bay Area. That includes Black Panther newspapers on microfilm, audio interviews with local civil rights activists and musicians, and the "Eternal Voices" video library with more than eighty years of African American East Bay history to discover—and that's just the library part. On the second floor, visitors can check out the museum that regularly hosts traveling and original exhibitions showcasing the art, history, and culture of African Americans. Note: The library is open Tuesdays through Saturdays from noon to 5:30 p.m.

659 14th Street
510-637-0200
oaklandlibrary.org/locations/african-american-museum-library-oakland

SIP HIGH TEA
AND EXPLORE PARDEE HOME MUSEUM

The Pardee Home Museum gives visitors a similar glimpse into Gold Rush history as San Francisco's historic Nob Hill. Built in 1868–69, the house's original owner, Enoch Pardee, moved to Oakland during the Gold Rush and became a respected eye doctor, later serving as mayor of Oakland, a state assemblyman, and state senator. His son, George C. Pardee, even became governor of California in 1902 and was praised for his leadership during the 1906 San Francisco earthquake. This influential history is matched by the beautiful Victorian architecture and at times bizarre collections on the interior. Governor Pardee's wife was a prestigious private collector, with more than seventy thousand objects still on display today. Candlesticks from India, rosaries from Mexico, and altar pieces from China are just a few of the gems visitors will find. In true fashion, High Tea can also be arranged at the property on any given day with an advanced reservation.

672 11th Street
510-444-2187
pardeehome.org

TIP

Visit Oakland's other popular historic house—
the Camron-Stanford House—
to experience the last of several mansions that
once surrounded Lake Merritt.

1418 Lakeside Drive, 510-974-7802,
cshouse.org

TAKE FLIGHT
AT OAKLAND AVIATION MUSEUM

Oakland had a major role in aviation as home to the Boeing School of Aeronautics, which was founded in 1929 by Boeing to compete with the Wright brothers' Wright Flying School and Curtiss Flying School in San Diego. The school started with one hundred students and swelled to include training of five thousand U.S. Army Mechanics during the height of World War II. The museum stands in the historic hangar built for the school in 1939. Not only does the building serve as a piece of history itself, but the museum also houses an extensive collection of aircraft, including the Cessna 0-2A flown in the Vietnam War to guide ground attack aircraft as well as the Short Solent Mk. III Flying Boat, one of only three of its kind remaining in the world today.

8252 Earhart Road
510-638-7100
oaklandaviationmuseum.org

DIYERS UNITE
AT NIMBY (NOT IN MY BACKYARD)

NIMBY provides a haven for DIYers looking for a place to get creative without worrying about complaints from landlords or neighbors. Now the largest do-it-yourself industrial space in the Bay Area, NIMBY is home to more than eighty different art groups and craftspeople with expertise in metal work, glass blowing, sculpting, and even custom car modifications. The studio spaces give artists access to tools and machines and can be used in a variety of ways. Some artists pay monthly fees for an art studio, while others can rent space for a single project in metal working, woodworking, or even recordings. People working on larger projects or exhibits can use the Gallery or Main Room spaces to host art shows or performances, even without having a regular space at NIMBY. Even those who aren't exactly hands-on can visit the space to discover some of the latest in Oakland artistry.

8410 Amelia Street
510-633-0506
nimbyspace.org

TRY A NARRATED WALKING TOUR
EXPLORING BLACK PANTHER PARTY HISTORY

Oakland has long been known for its contribution to the Civil Rights Movement, especially as the city where the Black Panther Party was founded by Dr. Huey Percy Newton and Bobby Seale. Even though that political passion continues today with civil rights protests happening regularly, visitors can get a glimpse of the city's political history by visiting famous Black Panther Party sites using a guided audio tour from Detour. You can simply download the audio tour in the Detour app and explore such sites as It's All Good Bakery, the North Oakland site that was once home of the Panthers' national headquarters.

5622 Martin Luther King Junior Way (Location of It's All Good Bakery)
detour.com/san-francisco/blackpanthers

SNAP A SHOT
OF THE MODERN CATHEDRAL
OF CHRIST THE LIGHT

Whether or not you're religious, the Cathedral of Christ the Light in downtown Oakland has become quite the photo-worthy structure ever since opening in 2008. Its modern, all-glass exterior and massive height quickly made it a landmark in the city skyline, especially as its reflection changes imagery and colors throughout the day. On the inside, the walls made of overlapping panels of wood and glass form a vault that mimics the scales of a fish in a design inspired by the "miracle of five loaves and two fish" biblical story. Known as the mother church for approximately 530,000 Catholics in Alameda and Contra Costa counties, it draws quite the crowds for masses held in English, Spanish, and Vietnamese throughout the week. It also offers free guided tours Monday through Friday for patrons to learn more about the Cathedral, its artwork, and the grounds.

2121 Harrison Street
510-832-5057
ctlcathedral.org

SEE WHAT'S HAPPENING
ON THE GREAT WALL OF OAKLAND

Strolling through downtown Oakland, you may happen to stumble upon a massive white wall that has become a centerpiece in the city's Uptown District. The Great Wall of Oakland is a nonprofit organization, and the 100-foot-by-100-foot projection installation brings free outdoor artwork to the community. The nonprofit focuses on supporting local artists to develop new work and then uses the wall to project that work during First Fridays or other special events. The wall also provides a space for the local Project Bandaloop to practice its aerial dance moves. Passersby can watch the dance troop seamlessly move about the wall several stories above downtown. Word to the wise: Always look up when walking down this part of West Grand because you never know what you might see.

West Grand Avenue (between Broadway and Valley Street)
greatwallofoakland.org

LEARN TRADITIONAL ASIAN DANCES
AT THE OAKLAND ASIAN CULTURAL CENTER

The Asian community is strong in Oakland, and nowhere is that more apparent than at the Oakland Asian Cultural Center (OACC). Opened in 1996 in the heart of Chinatown, the OACC offers workshops, classes, performances, exhibitions, and even performances for anyone to learn more about Asian culture and heritage. South Indian dance, Mongolian dance, and Chinese folk dance classes and performances mix with art, cooking, and Mandarin classes. Rotating exhibits also pay tribute to this community and culture that continues to have a strong influence in the city. That includes the public festivals the OACC presents throughout the year: Lunar New Year Festival in February and the Asian Pacific American Heritage Festival in May.

388 9th Street, Suite 290
510-637-0455
oacc.cc

Photo Credit:
Jessie Fetterling

SHOPPING AND FASHION

KEEP IT FRESH
AT GRAND LAKE FARMERS MARKET

Grand Lake Farmers Market is not your average farmers market—even by Bay Area standards. The Saturday market is open year-round from 9:00 a.m. to 2:00 p.m. and features produce from more than forty local farmers, thirty specialty food purveyors, and a handful of local artisans. But it's much more than that. The Grand Lake Farmers Market has become part of a routine for most residents. It's not just about picking up fresh fruits and veggies but being a part of the local scene. Its close proximity to Lake Merritt also gives it an advantage, making it almost impossible to pass on a warm Oakland day. As the market continues to grow in popularity, it has started to swell beyond its general location, with other vendors and artisans selling goods along the sidewalks to and from the market.

Lake Park Avenue
415-472-6100
argiculturalinstitute.org

Also check out:

Old Oakland Farmers' Market (on Fridays)
9th Street at Broadway
510-745-7100
uvfm.org/old-oakland-fridays

Temescal Farmers' Market (on Sundays)
5300 Claremont Avenue
510-745-7100
uvfm.org/temescal-sunday

SHOP FOR JEWELRY
AT ESQUELETO

Some of Oakland's best shopping can be found in North Oakland's Temescal District—specifically Temescal Alley and Alley 49. These two pedestrian alleys are lined by locally owned specialty shops, including Esqueleto, an eclectic jewelry store that offers a wide range of designers. You can buy everything here, from a simple pair of earrings to engagement and wedding rings. Small bios of the designers accompany the jewelry-lined cases, so you get a sense of the heart and energy that went into each specially designed piece. In addition to jewelry, the store sells high-end knickknacks that make the interiors oh so inviting. The store's website has even more options and features fun suggestions, such as Staff Picks and a Stack of the Week, which includes rings from the store's various designers stacked together for an innovative jewelry combo.

482 A 49th Street
410-629-6216
shopesqueleto.com

PICK UP A PLANT
AT CRIMSON HORTICULTURAL RARITIES

Walk about a hundred feet east of Esqueleto to the start of Temescal Alley, and you will find this gem of a plant shop that provides the cozy comfort of a greenhouse. An unusual assortment of indoor plants come in a variety of shapes and sizes, both loose and even mounted to objects for hanging. This combined with the wide selection of decorative pots make it an ideal place to grab a gift or get crafty with your own personal home décor. While not exactly cheap, the plants are well maintained, and the staff is knowledgeable in all things gardening. Mix in the store's selection of candles, soaps, and gardening books to create the ideal Sunday afternoon shopping excursion. A personal favorite: the shop's extensive air plants.

470 49th Street
510-992-3359
crimsonhort.com

DISCOVER LOCAL ARTISANS
AT OAKLANDISH

Oakland pride is on display at Oaklandish Downtown Shop, where visitors will find a variety of local clothing and accessories that celebrate all that makes Oakland great. While the retail store touts the Oaklandish fashion line—featuring designs that honor the area's beloved sports teams to the company's classic oak tree logo for which the city is named—it also supplies the community with a wide array of local artisanal goods. Spices, sauces, artwork, and even books by local authors line the tables in this popular downtown store. Plus, their "local love" slogan rings true with a portion of proceeds supporting grassroots organizations. Note: This downtown location is just one of the Oaklandish brand's locations.

1444 Broadway
510-251-9500
oaklandish.com

Also visit:

Oaklandish Dimond Shop
3419 Fruitvale Avenue
510-482-2020
oaklandish.com

Oakland Supply Co.
427 Water Street
510-817-4488
oaklandish.com

RATTO'S MARKET & DELI Since 1897

Caffe 817

Photo Credit:
Jessie Fetterling

EXPERIENCE A HISTORIC MARKET
AT RATTO'S

Ratto's International Market & Deli is a fourth-generation, family-owned and -operated market first opened in 1897 by Giovanni Battista (G.B.) Ratto in the neighborhood now known as Old Oakland. The historic shop was one of the first grocery stores in the Bay Area to offer Mediterranean spices, bulk rice, pasta, and Italian olive oils. As such, customers would travel sometimes a couple of hours to buy the ingredients needed to prepare their traditional family recipes. The market still serves a wide variety of bulk spices, Ratto's own vinegar, olive oils, and pastas in addition to a curated selection of wines, cheeses, and salamis. The deli offers a wide selection of signature sandwiches, including a classic Italian combo on ciabatta bread. To add to the family feel, the husband of current owner Elena Durante, G.B.'s great-granddaughter, plays the jazz piano every Saturday in the back of the market.

821 Washington Street
510-832-6503
rattos.com

READ A MAGAZINE (OR TWENTY)
AT ISSUES

Print is not dead at this shop completely dedicated to magazines. Located right off popular Piedmont Avenue, Issues is a godsend to magazine enthusiasts (and publishers) everywhere. Its hip atmosphere makes reading cool again in the same way that record stores are glorifying vinyl. Readers can similarly spend hours searching through its extensive collection of national and international magazines. While it carries the typical *Vogue* and *National Geographic,* it also carries other niche titles that have become impossible to find in stores. Other paper products, such as greeting cards, stationary, a wide variety of newspapers, and a small stash of books, are also available. (And, yes, true to its trendy nature, the store has some records for sale, too.)

20 Glen Avenue
510-652-5700
issuesshop.com

TASTE YOUR WAY
THROUGH ROCKRIDGE MARKET HALL

Locals are jealous of the lucky residents that live near and get to frequent Rockridge Market Hall in the popular neighborhood of the same name. The high-end, European-style market features imported goods for patrons hoping to get their hands on authentic Italian olive oil or French chocolates. International customers looking for a taste of home will especially love the cheese and cured meat sections, with an abundance of options on display. These culinary delights are sold alongside house-stuffed sausages and loaves of bread made fresh in the market bakery. Even the Highwire Coffee Roasters coffee here is top-notch, since it is roasted and blended on-site. The market also hosts culinary events, such as tastings and book signings by famous food authors.

5655 College Avenue, Suite 201
510-250-6000
rockridgemarkethall.com

SNIFF YOUR WAY
THROUGH OAKTOWN SPICE SHOP

A culinary wizard's ultimate playground, Oaktown Spice Shop doles out a wide variety of spices, herbs, and hand-mixed blends. When you walk into the shop, it's difficult to decide which area to check out first, but the wall dedicated solely to peppercorns is a good place to start. Or the aromatic seeds on display might be more up your alley. Either way, prepare yourself for an afternoon of new smells, such as the Better Than Everything Bagel Spice—the shop's own version of seasoning that makes or breaks the popular breakfast food. Black truffle sea salt, Saigon cinnamon, Jamaican curry powder, and other rare finds are what make this one of the top spice shops in the Bay Area and possibly the country.

546 Grand Avenue
510-201-5400
oaktownspiceshop.com

MIX AND MATCH SCENTS
AT BODY TIME

If you've ever had an interest in the art of perfumery, then Body Time is the place for you. This body shop allows you to customize your own scent by mixing and matching different perfumes and essential oils that cater to your personal preference. Once you've found your scent, you can have staff members mix it with one of the store's unscented bath or body products. Most of the available scents—Holy Basil or German Chamomile to name two—are unisex so that both male and female customers can feel confident choosing a personalized smell. What started in Berkeley in 1970 has grown into several East Bay locations, with this one in Oakland's Rockridge neighborhood.

5521 College Avenue
510-547-5116
bodytime.com

FIND DECADENT KNICKKNACKS
AT MAISON D'ETRE

Every home should include something from Maison d'Etre—even if you can only afford a simple piece of glassware. True to its French essence, the shop's home furnishings are of the utmost quality, with pillows costing in the hundreds. But as you move through the narrow walkways in this home goods store, you'll find a wide range of knickknacks that cater to every price point. Cookbooks mix with decadent flatware, while pillows line shelves next to jewelry displays—each one as uniquely beautiful as the next. The tiny shop is so packed with trinkets waiting to be taken home that you'll forget you're in Oakland until you emerge outside with something in hand.

5640 College Avenue
510-658-2801
maisondetre.com

PERUSE THE ARTISAN-MADE GOODS
AT KOSA ARTS

The floor-to-ceiling windows that make up Kosa Arts' storefront invite customers inside, but its wide variety of goods are what keep people here. Kosa Arts sells home goods, apparel, and art that are so well crafted it's like walking through an art gallery more than a boutique. Everything from the wooden furniture to the decadent chocolate to the hand-dyed tops was chosen just for this shop. While not everything in the store is made locally in Oakland, the shop continues to help engage the Oakland arts community with special fashion events and by participating in Oakland First Fridays.

386 19th Street
510-394-2752
kosaarts.com

SUPPORT LOCAL ATHLETICS
AT BEAST MODE

Local athletic hero Marshawn Lynch, a professional running back who played for the Seattle Seahawks before returning home to play for the Oakland Raiders football team, put his money where his mouth is by starting a clothing line. Lynch named the line Beast Mode, the nickname he received for his powerful running style, and has since opened two retail stores of the same name. The first opened in the heart of downtown Oakland, and the other is, fittingly, located in Seattle. The line includes athletic gear for men, women, and children, as well as accessories, such as water bottles and hats.

811 Broadway
510-908-2195
beastmodeonline.com

GET SOME KICKS
AT SOLESPACE

Equal parts shoe store and art gallery, SoleSpace is a creative lab that truly combines the art and fashion communities in Oakland. It was founded in 2012 featuring high-end lifestyle footwear, including such brands as Adidas, CLAE, and Miz Mooz. While customers come to browse the goods by day, SoleSpace turns into an innovative event space at night. Past events included a #DubzAgainstTheWorld Art Exhibit by Conscious Basketball, featuring Golden State Warriors–themed artwork. Oakland First Fridays are especially popular here, with local designers being featured. Note: Make sure to visit later in the day, as the store opens at noon on weekdays and at 11:00 a.m. on weekends.

1714 Telegraph Avenue
510-306-1585
solespace.myshopify.com

TIP

Check out SoleSpace's flagship
retail location as well.

3304 Grand Avenue, 510-306-1585,
solespace.myshopify.com

FLIP THROUGH THE VINYL SELECTION
AT 1-2-3-4 GO! RECORDS

This record store has a fresh, inviting look, welcoming vinyl enthusiasts to spend hours flipping through records. Its red walls and funky décor—an old telephone booth and wooden movie-theater seats—create a retro feel to match the wide range (with an emphasis on punk music) of used records on sale. Even though the store prides itself in buying used records for a fair cost, it also sells a great many new ones just waiting to be played for the first time. Michael Jackson's *Thriller* album is mixed in with ones from hip-hop artists, such as Frank 'n' Dank. Unlike most record stores in the Bay Area, 1-2-3-4 Go! Records even has enough space to host live music several nights of the week. Note: It also has a location in San Francisco's Mission District.

420 40th Street, #5
510-985-0325
1234gorecords.com

PICK UP ESSENTIAL OILS OR EARRINGS
AT FIELD DAY AND FRIENDS

Field Day offers everything from clothes to jewelry to handmade soaps—about eighty percent of which are all made locally in Oakland by owner Trinity Cross and her friends. While its storefront is small, you could spend a serious amount of time here perusing the shop's carefully curated selection of sustainable goods. Its line of clothing, for instance, is designed, cut, sewn, dyed, and finished in town. And then its entire wall dedicated to earrings, handcrafted by local jewelers as well as a few friends from throughout the Pacific Northwest, makes it difficult to commit to just one pair. Essential oils, soaps, and handcrafted greeting cards round out the goods one can expect to find in this gem of a store.

329 19th Street
510-338-6624
fielddayapparel.com

DECORATE YOUR HOME
WITH GOODS FROM NEIGHBOR

Neighbor is a collaboration between the owners of nearby Good Stock and Mercy Vintage in Piedmont. Both California natives, Dana Olson (owner of Good Stock) and Karen Anderson-Fort (owner of Mercy Vintage) bring their eye for design to this carefully curated home décor store. Hand-woven baskets, decorative rugs, and colorful pillows mix in with lotions, jewelry, and wooden spoons. Make your way to the store's backyard, where succulents abound, and other trinkets can be found in the inviting wooden alcove out back. Before you know it, you'll be making excuses as to why you need certain items for your house. If not, the cheerful staff will do it for you.

4200 Piedmont Avenue
510-594-2288
iloveneighbor.com

TIP

Don't forget to check out Dana and Karen's other boutiques on the same block in Piedmont. Good Stock features high-end jewelry, bags, and beauty products, while Mercy Vintage offers a wide variety of vintage and high-end designer clothing.

Good Stock, 4198 Piedmont Avenue, 510-653-8518, wearegoodstock.com
Mercy Vintage, 4188 Piedmont Avenue, 510-654-5599, mercyvintage.com

CHECK OUT
YOUR LOCAL LAUREL BOOK STORE

Laurel Book Store is proof that independent book stores, at least in the Bay Area, are still thriving. What started in 2001 as a nine-hundred-square-foot store in the city's Laurel district has expanded into a store four times its original size in downtown's landmark 1907 Lionel J. Wilson Building. While the book store has an inviting display of books, its support of the community is what makes it so popular. Not only does it host monthly book clubs for readers, but it also hosts a wide range of other events, from book launch parties to author readings. It even supports local causes by occasionally donating portions of its sales. To stay ahead of the times, it even partners with companies to bring customers audiobooks and the like.

1423 Broadway
510-452-9232
laurelbookstore.com

Three Other Book Stores to Peruse:

East Bay Booksellers
5433 College Avenue
510-653-9965
ebbooksellers.com

Pegasus Books Oakland
5560 College Avenue
510-652-6259
pegasusbookstore.com

Walden Pond Books
3316 Grand Avenue
510-832-4438
waldenpondbooks.com

Photo Credit:
Esqueleto

SUGGESTED
ITINERARIES

DATE NIGHT

Camino, 13

Morcom Rose Garden, 78

New Parkway Theater, The, 53

LADIES WEEKEND

Body Time, 118

Esqueleto, 107

Field Day and Friends, 125

Mua, 14

Oakland Urban Wine Trail, 34

Overland Country Bar & Grill, 56

Somar Bar and Lounge, 55

FUN FOR THE FAM

California Canoe & Kayak, 69

Chabot Space and Science Center, 87

Children's Fairyland, 63

Crown Memorial State Beach, 81

Fentons Creamery, 12

Lake Merritt, 62

Museum of Children's Arts, 92

Oakland Zoo, 75

Plank, 71

ON A BUDGET

NEAR THE CONVENTION CENTER

Photo Credit:
Wild Within Studio

ACTIVITIES
BY SEASON

SPRING

Children's Fairyland, 63

California Canoe & Kayak, 69

Ferry from Jack London Square, 80

Mountain View Cemetery, 65

Sibley Volcanic Regional Preserve, 73

SUMMER

Crown Memorial State Beach, 81

Fentons Creamery, 12

Great Wall of Oakland, The, 100

Lake Merritt, 62

Morcom Rose Garden, 78

Woodminster Amphitheater, 57

FALL

Grand Lake Farmers Market, 104

Joaquin Miller Park, 68

Oakland First Fridays, 84

Oakland Zoo, 75

Piedmont Springs, 70

WINTER

INDEX